RUBANK BOOK OF FLUTE SOLOS
EASY LEVEL

Printable Piano Accompaniments

PLAYBACK+
Speed • Pitch • Balance • Loop

CONTENTS

To access recordings and PDF accompaniments visit:
www.halleonard.com/mylibrary

Enter Code
5796-5347-3591-5115

ISBN 978-1-4950-6502-6

RUBANK®

HAL•LEONARD® CORPORATION
7777 W. BLUEMOUND RD. P.O. BOX 13819 MILWAUKEE, WI 53213

Visit Hal Leonard Online at
www.halleonard.com

Bourree And Menuet

From "Flute Sonata No. III"

Flute

G.F. Handel
Edited by H. Voxman

Elegie
Op. 55, No. 1

Flute

Joachim Andersen
Edited by H. Voxman

Gavotte

From "Don Juan"

Flute

C.W. von Gluck
Transcribed by H. Voxman

First Waltz

Flute

A. Gretchaninoff
Transcribed by H. Voxman

Gavotte

Flute

Fr. Jos. Gossec
Edited by H. Voxman

The Lonely Birch Tree

Russian Folk Song

Flute

Arranged by
Clarence E. Hurrell

Menuett Paysanne

Flute

W.A. Mozart
Transcribed by H. Voxman

Petite Gavotte

Flute

G.F. Handel
Transcribed by H. Voxman

Round Dance

Flute

Franz Schubert
Transcribed by H. Voxman

Spirit Dance

From The Opera "Orpheus"

Flute

C.W. von Gluck
Transcribed by H. Voxman

Two Russian Songs

Flute

N. Miaskovsky
Transcribed by H. Voxman

A. Goedicke
Transcribed by H. Voxman

Song Without Words

Op. 37, No.1

Flute

M. Hauser
Arranged by Adolf Hass

Valse Petite

Flute

Arline Hinkson